Dragsters

SPORT

BY DENNY VON FINN

AMALIE
MOTOR OIL

TORQUE
TM

BELLWETHER MEDIA • MINNEAPOLIS, MN

TORQUE ™

Are you ready to take it to the extreme? Torque books thrust you into the action-packed world of sports, vehicles, and adventure. These books may include dirt, smoke, fire, and dangerous stunts.

WARNING: READ AT YOUR OWN RISK.

This edition first published in 2009 by Bellwether Media.

No part of this publication may be reproduced in whole or in part without written permission of the publisher. For information regarding permission, write to Bellwether Media Inc., Attention: Permissions Department, Post Office Box 19349, Minneapolis, MN 55419.

Library of Congress Cataloging-in-Publication Data
Von Finn, Denny.
  Dragsters / by Denny Von Finn.
      p. cm. — (Torque. Cool rides)
  Includes bibliographical references and index.
  Summary: "Amazing photography accompanies engaging information about Dragsters. The combination of high-interest subject matter and light text is intended for readers in grades 3 through 7"—Provided by publisher.
  ISBN-13: 978-1-60014-209-3 (hardcover : alk. paper)
  ISBN-10: 1-60014-209-5 (hardcover : alk. paper)
  1. Dragsters—Juvenile literature. I. Title.

TL236.2.V66 2009
629.228—dc22   2008017016

Contents

What Is a Dragster?

Dragsters are unique race cars. They are long and low. Some are more than 25 feet (7.6 meters) long. Dragsters have large rear tires. Their front tires are skinny, like a bicycle's. However, don't let their strange looks fool you. They are tremendously powerful.

The fastest dragsters
reach speeds of 330 miles
(531 kilometers) per hour.
These high speeds make
dragsters one of the most
popular race cars in the
United States.

Fast FaCt

A Top Fuel dragster consumes
1.5 gallons (5.7 liters) of fuel
per second.

Dragster History

Organized drag racing started after World War II. Many soldiers learned about engines and vehicles during the war. When they came home, they modified their cars for racing.

These early racers knew that lighter cars were faster. They removed unnecessary parts from their cars. The lighter vehicles looked as skinny as railroad tracks. The early dragsters were known as **rail jobs**.

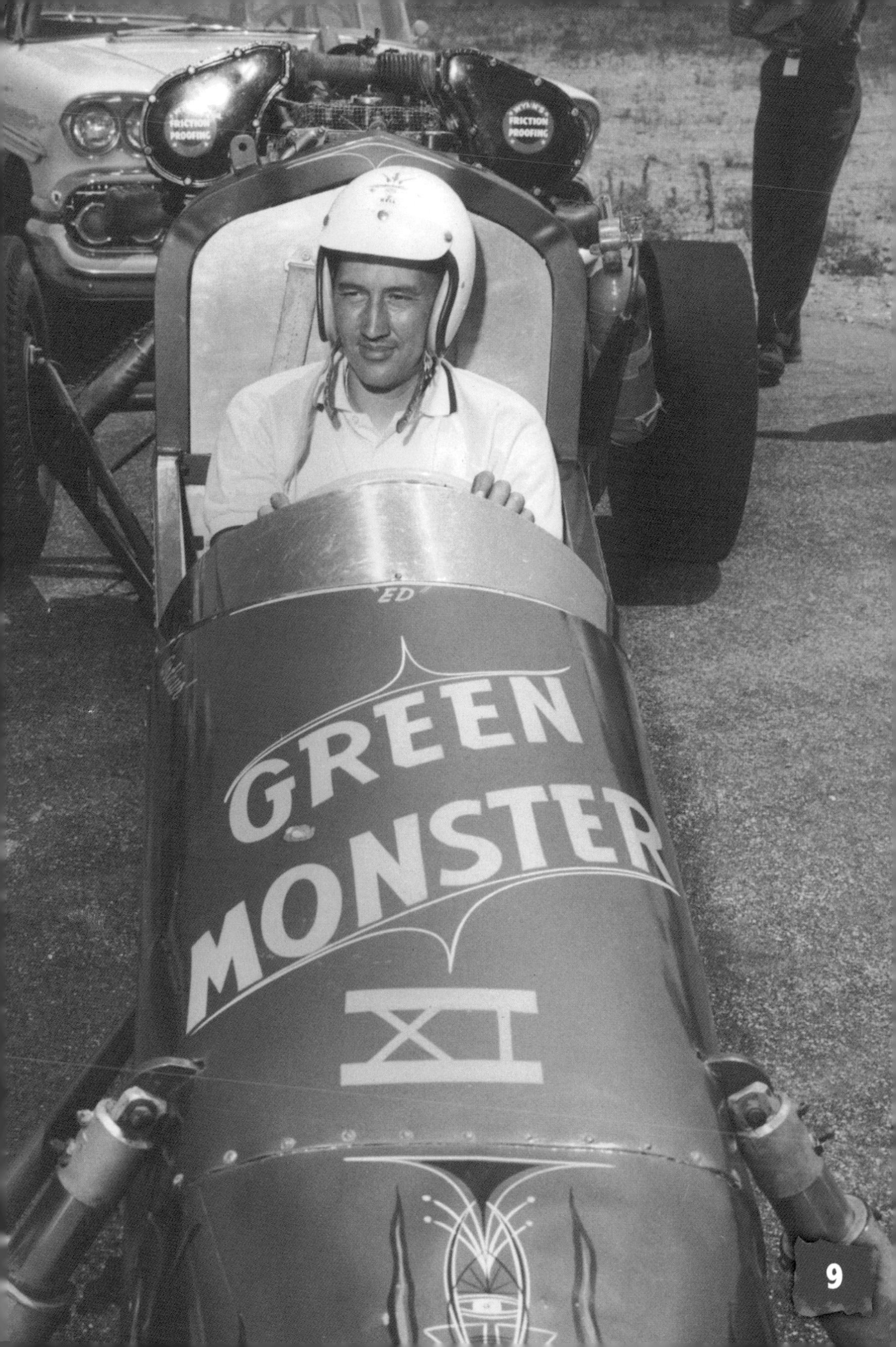
FRICTION PROOFING
FRICTION PROOFING
ED
GREEN MONSTER
XI

The first legal drag races were held at a California airport in 1949. In 1951, Wally Parks formed the National Hot Rod Association (NHRA). He wanted to promote safe drag racing. Thanks to Parks, drag racing became even more popular. The NHRA still sponsors drag racing today.

Parts of a Dragster

Dragsters use powerful engines called **Top Fuel** engines. Top Fuel engines are among the most powerful machines on Earth.

They use **nitromethane** and alcohol instead of gasoline. These engines can produce up to 7,500 **horsepower**! Inside, they reach 2,400 degrees Fahrenheit (760 degrees Celsius).

Such powerful engines can be extremely dangerous. Some have even been known to explode. A blanket called a **diaper** surrounds the engine's oil pan. The diaper is made of the same material as bullet-proof vests. It protects the driver in case of an explosion.

Fast FaCt

Team members must completely rebuild Top Fuel dragster engines after each run; they can do this in less than 30 minutes.

The smooth rear tires of a dragster are called **slicks**. They are made of rubber. Drivers perform **burnouts** before races to heat their slicks. The rubber becomes sticky. This helps the tires grip the pavement.

Downforce also helps a dragster grip the pavement. A dragster has **foils** in the front and back. As a dragster gains speed, air passing over the wing-like foils pushes the dragster down.

Dragsters in Action

Dragsters race one-on-one. Each car moves to the starting line. The rumbling of the engines shakes the ground! Three yellow lights blink on the **Christmas tree**. Then the green light flashes. The cars are off in a deafening roar. The **dragstrip** is straight and 0.25 miles (0.4 kilometers) long. The race only lasts about 5 seconds.

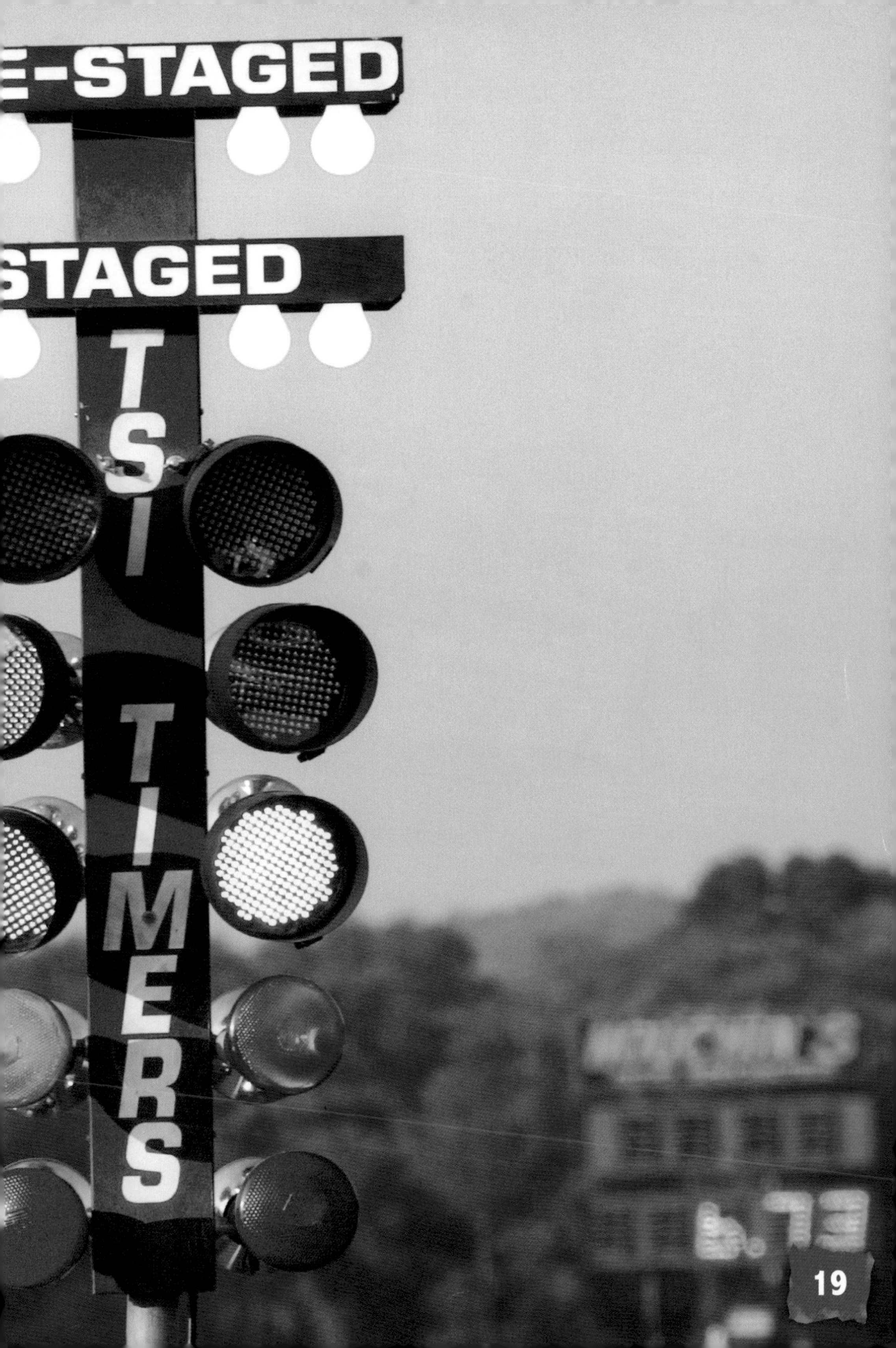
E-STAGED
STAGED
TSI
TIMERS

The cars cross the finish line. **Chutes** pop open behind them. The losing dragster is eliminated from competition.

The winning dragster will race the winner of another match-up.

Fast FaCt

In 2007, a scientist measured the ground-disturbance from a Top Fuel dragster. He learned it was equal to a medium-sized earthquake!

Eventually, only two cars will remain to race for top honors. The winner will be crowned champion.

Glossary

burnout—the act of spinning tires before a race to heat them for better traction

Christmas tree—a tower of bright yellow, green, and red lights that signal the start of a drag race

chute—a parachute that helps a dragster stop at the end of a race

diaper—an extra-strong blanket that protects the driver in case of an engine explosion

downforce—a physical force that pushes a dragster toward the pavement

dragstrip—the race track for dragsters

foils—the wing-like parts of a dragster that help create downforce

horsepower—a unit for measuring the power of an engine

nitromethane—an explosive liquid that helps power Top Fuel dragsters

rail jobs—long, thin dragsters with no body panels

slicks—wide, smooth racing tires

Top Fuel—the name given to today's fastest dragsters

To Learn More

AT THE LIBRARY

Doeden, Matt. *Dragsters*. Mankato, Minn.: Capstone, 2003.

Werther, Scott P. *Dragsters*. New York: Powerkids, 2002.

Zuehlke, Jeffrey and Dick Licata. *Drag Racers*. Minneapolis, Minn.: Lerner, 2008.

ON THE WEB

Learning more about dragsters

is as easy as 1, 2, 3.

1. Go to www.factsurfer.com

2. Enter "dragsters" into search box.

3. Click the "Surf" button and you will
   see a list of related web sites.

With factsurfer.com, finding more information is just a click away.

Index

The images in this book are reproduced through the courtesy of: Robert Clayton / Alamy, front cover, pp. 13, 14-15; picturesbyrob / Alamy, pp. 4-5, 16-17; Robert Young/ Getty Images, pp. 6-7; Carsten / Getty Images, pp. 8-9; FPG / Getty Images, pp. 10-11; zoomstock / Masterfile, p. 12; Wm. Baker/Getty Images, p. 19; Tony Watson / Alamy, pp. 20-21.